THE UNIQUE CHARACTER OF AMERICAN SECONDARY EDUCATION

LONDON : HUMPHREY MILFORD

OXFORD UNIVERSITY PRESS

The Inglis Lecture, 1928

THE UNIQUE CHARACTER OF AMERICAN SECONDARY EDUCATION

BY

CHARLES HUBBARD JUDD
University of Chicago

CAMBRIDGE
HARVARD UNIVERSITY PRESS
1928

THE
INGLIS LECTURESHIP

To honor the memory of Alexander Inglis, 1879–1924, his friends and colleagues gave to the Graduate School of Education, Harvard University, a fund for the maintenance of a Lectureship in Secondary Education. To the study of problems in this field Professor Inglis devoted his professional career, leaving as a precious heritage to his co-workers the example of his industry, intellectual integrity, human sympathy, and social vision. It is the purpose of the Lectureship to perpetuate the spirit of his labors and contribute to the solution of problems in the field of his interest. The lectures on this foundation are published annually by the School.

THE UNIQUE CHARACTER OF AMERICAN SECONDARY EDUCATION

CHARLES HUBBARD JUDD
UNIVERSITY OF CHICAGO

A FRIEND of mine who is the principal of an elementary school on the West Side of Chicago, near the stockyards, tells me that some years ago there came into his office a Bohemian who introduced himself in broken English as the father of one of the boys in the school. The father said that his son, who was in the eighth grade, was being encouraged by his teacher to enter high school. He wanted to know whether it was true that the boy could go to high school. The principal assured him that it was and added the comment that the boy was bright and was doing very well in his school work. Thinking that it might be necessary to persuade the father, the principal began to describe the advantages of a high-school education. The Bohemian, who knew only Old World ways, interrupted the principal by asking, "What will it cost me to have the boy go to high school?" "Nothing," was the reply. "Excuse me," said the Bohemian father, "I do not understand English very well." It required several repetitions to convince him that in America the opportunity of a higher education is open to every boy who finishes the eighth grade — and that without cost.

The counterpart of this incident recently appeared in press dispatches from France. Two statements which were published in American newspapers in October of this year may be quoted. The first is as follows:

M. Herriot, the French minister of education, has given notice of his intention to make education in the *lycées* free. The methods by which he intends to carry out this proposal will be submitted to the finance committee of the chamber. The adoption of this reform, which will involve credits estimated at 58,000,000 f., can only be carried out in successive stages. For this year several hundred thousand francs only will be asked in order to insure free secondary education in the colleges where a fusion has already been effected with the higher primary education. M. Poincaré has given his assent to the financial measures involved in this proposal.

The second statement tells what French editorial writers said with regard to the proposal of the minister of education.

Minister of Education Edouard Herriot's proposal to make institutions of higher learning accessible to the poor as well as the rich by offering free tuition, as is done in most American state universities, caused strong protest in Conservative circles.

At present it takes a considerable sum to go through the universities. About the only poor students able to do it are those who win scholarships.

"It will ruin French culture and flood the universities with those who ought to be carpenters and day laborers, and give us a host of third-rate journalists, lawyers, doctors, and politicians," the Conservative papers *Le Temps* and *Journal des Débats* say.

Turning from France to England, we find ample evidence on which to base a contrast between conditions in America and in England. The London *Times Educational Supplement* of July 23, 1927, has a leading article dealing with the difficulties encountered by many pupils in securing a secondary education. Americans perhaps need to have their attention called explicitly to the fact that attendance on a secondary school in England is possible only when someone pays for the pupil's tuition. The following are the opening paragraphs of the

Times article; they will be fully understood only when the facts regarding tuition requirements are kept in mind.

With the increased demand for, and provision of, secondary education, the number of young people is also increasing whose education or professional training is threatened by reason of lack of means. Only a few win scholarships substantial enough to insure the completion of their training, and schoolmasters and schoolmistresses are again and again called upon to suggest sources of help other than those based on purely competitive examinations for students who have got some way, and for whom it seems a pity not to go farther. Most of the general societies that exist for this purpose have already more applications than they can possibly meet, and there is often not very much hope for a candidate unless through some professional or local society whose resources may not be quite so strained or on which the applicant may for some reason have some priority of call.

All societies, however, consider cases on their merits; and the head of a school who has the interests of boys and girls at heart will seldom leave any stone unturned. Since the expenditure of these loan funds is practically all productive expenditure, the results of which can be almost immediately measured in terms of hard work and happiness, they should appeal to all persons of good will with money to give or leave, and it is a pity that the fear of being overwhelmed by applications which they cannot meet should drive so many of the existing organizations into a semi-retirement where they are little heard of. The Charity Organization Society (296 Vauxhall Bridge-road) has access to many of them and catalogues them with other sources of help in its *Annual Charities Register and Digest*. The following particulars, however, have been for the most part obtained by personal investigation and by the courtesy of the secretaries of the various societies and funds.

Following these paragraphs is a full front page of the *Times Educational Supplement* listing sources of aid for worthy young people who want to attend secondary schools.

Another example which shows the

contrast between European and American conditions is drawn from my own experience. Some years ago I was visiting schools in Hamburg. A German friend who knew that I was anxious to gain a full understanding of the German educational system took me to a private school which received boys who had not been allowed to go on in the *Gymnasium* because they had been adjudged to be failures in their courses. I talked with the teachers in this private school and with some of the boys. It appeared that most of the boys came from homes of the merchant class. The parents were able to pay for the schooling of their sons and had sent them to the *Gymnasium* in the hope that they might rise out of the social rank in which they were born into the professional and governing classes of society. The boys had failed and were cut off from advancement to higher ranks in society because the doors to professional study and to social preferment are open only to those who pass through the *Gymnasium*. What interested me was the statement repeatedly made that these boys were competent enough intellectually but the teachers in the *Gymnasium* had deliberately excluded them from the opportunity of further study because the professions were overcrowded and it was not desired that the merchant class should break through the social defenses which surrounded aristocratic exclusiveness.

One more reference to happenings on the other side of the Atlantic and the point which I wish to make is, I think, clearly proved. Sweden recently adopted a new school code. This code substitutes for the long-established educational system which gave to only a favored few the opportunity of securing a secondary education, a new system in which access to secondary education is offered to all who complete the work of the common school.

The cases which I have cited were not chosen with a view to emphasizing the well-known fact that American high schools are accessible to pupils from all levels of society. They were chosen with the purpose of emphasizing the fact that everywhere in the modern world there is an eager desire on the part of pupils and their parents for a share in the advantages of higher education. The German merchant class desires an education higher than that which is provided in the *Volksschule*. The French minister of education feels the pressure from the common people. England hears the voices of many who are now excluded from her secondary schools asking even in the name of charity for a privilege universally desired.

There are those who are critical of the American high school because its doors are open to pupils of all types. The critics of the American system write elaborate treatises in order to convince us that our program of free universal secondary education is a failure. For my part, I am convinced that the experiment which America is trying cannot be abandoned for the simple reason that human nature here and in every other country is eagerly seeking access to higher education. That the American high school is accessible to all classes in society is a result of the fact that the desires of the common people come more readily to expression under the conditions of American life than under the rigid conditions of older social orders. European countries, bound by the traditions of the past, are slowly beginning to demand for all the people what America has long provided. Even if our plan were to fail, the trend toward universal secondary education is so strong that other countries would carry on the undertaking.

I do not understand how anyone who studies the obvious trends in the world's educational systems can suggest that the United States turn backward. It is the duty of our people to examine critically the results of the experiment of developing secondary education in which this country is engaged, but we should never be misled by cynical critics into thinking that we are behind Europe. The day will certainly come when the French *lycée* will be free and when Germany will have, as Sweden now has, that which has been discussed long and vigorously, a high school open to all who complete the elementary curriculum. Those in Germany who look forward to this broader educational opportunity call the school for which they hope the *Einheitsschule*. In England they have a picturesque name for the school system to-

ward which they are moving. Some day
England will arrive at the goal for which
the common people are striving and will
have its "end-on" school. Then boys
and girls from the board school will not
depend on charity for the right to pass
from the common school into higher
institutions.

When I speak of the American high
school as an experiment, I do not mean
at all to imply that it is a questionable or
temporary undertaking. Every great
social movement is an experiment in
human adaptation. There is certainly
no reason for discouragement in the fact
that the lines along which we have been
innovating are not altogether clear. We,
like every generation before us, are ex-
perimenting with life, and the degree of
perfection which we attain will depend
quite as much on our courage to make
progressive changes as on our critical in-
sight with regard to our defects. If we

need to renew our courage, we have only to look about us and to note that the ideal toward which we are striving is beginning to be accepted by nations that are much less advanced than are we in experimentation with secondary education.

The secondary schools of the world are outgrowths of the urge for higher things; they are also in a peculiar sense reflections of the social and economic conditions in the countries in which they exist. Elementary schools are much alike in all civilized countries. The secondary schools and the universities of a nation are the institutions which give distinctive character to its educational system. We can understand secondary schools only when we understand the social system of which they are a part.

The conditions of life in Europe are so thoroughly systematized that the individual has little or no escape from the

classifications imposed on him by in-
heritance. A boy born in the peasant
class in any of the European countries
will continue to be a peasant all his days.
The artisan's son expects to enter upon
some trade closely related to that which
his father follows. Much of the efficiency
of Europeans is due to the fact that
whole families carry on from generation
to generation the same industrial opera-
tions and hand down from father to son
the wisdom of experience. At the levels
above the peasant and artisan classes,
the son of professional or aristocratic
parents is obligated by social expectation
to maintain the traditions of his family
and class.

In contrast with all this is the outlook
on life of an American youth. It is not
at all the uniform expectation in the
United States that a boy will do what his
father did before him or that a girl will
imitate her mother. If there is one char-

acteristic more conspicuous than another in an American, it is his determina-
tion to seek the adventure of a career
which has never been followed by any of
his forebears. The possibility of migration to new parts of the country, the
rapid development of new industries, the
opening up of a host of new professions,
have created on this continent a movement in our population and a variety
of experiments in personal adaptation
which have no parallel in the older civi-
lizations.

It is quite unthinkable that American
schools should develop their programs
of instruction uninfluenced by the conditions which have been described. Un-
certainty as to a pupil's future creates a
unique problem. It is very easy to pre-
scribe a curriculum for a boy who is
stamped by heredity with an indelible
mark, as is the European boy. It is a
very different matter to arrange courses

of study for a boy who may be a plumber or who may equally well be a legislator.

The American high school has been organized with a view to providing for pupils who do not expect to follow in the footsteps of their fathers. It has as one of its chief characteristics a flexibility which no other secondary school in the world exhibits.

If one is critical of the unsettled conditions in American life, one is likely to view the extreme flexibility of our schools with a feeling of dismay if not with utter despair. One may even advocate, as some recent writers have done, a reversion to the substantial and rigid organization of European schools. There is something consoling about the immobile curriculum and the ancient customs of European institutions. One cannot but admire the secondary schools of England, where gentlemen have lived together for centuries. One must respect the *Gym-*

nasien of Germany, which stand as the narrow gateways to those great scientific centers, the German universities. One is justified in being envious of the French *lycées*, where perfect style is cultivated and logic is transmitted. It is little wonder that many who are disturbed by the coming and going in our western civilization should look on European education as so much more compact than anything which we have, that they would fain induce us to adopt the *Gymnasium* and the *lycée* as models on which to pattern our future.

It has come to be quite the custom for critics of American education to make hasty excursions to Europe, sometimes in person, sometimes in imagination, and to come back with descriptions of what ought to be done in America. I never read these exhortations to be like Europe without thinking of the fundamental differences in the life of the two continents which make real imitation utterly impossible. Europe has social castes. European education grew from above downward. European secondary schools were in the past and are in very large measure today the homes of aristocracy, accessible only to the élite. American education grew from below upward. The high school of this country is a part of the common-school system, and into it come great groups of young people who have no definite ideas as to the callings which they will follow in later life. Much less do these young people know what stations in society they are ultimately to occupy.

American ingenuity is heavily taxed to meet the demand for an educational device which is at once efficient and sufficiently flexible to provide for the training of the unsettled youth of this country. Two experiments have been launched to meet the demand for flexibility. One is

the cosmopolitan high school. The other
is the elective system.

The cosmopolitan high school is an
effort to concentrate under one roof instruction in all the lines which may under any conditions be required for the
preparation of secondary-school pupils
for life. The special academic school or
the special trade school does not provide
the individual pupil with a ready opportunity for a broad training, as does the
school in which all subjects are administered as parts of a single cosmopolitan
plan.

The elective system is an administrative device for allowing the individual
pupil the largest possible liberty to come
in contact with as many and as diverse
phases of experience as the school can
provide.

I am not concerned at the moment
either to condemn or to defend the cosmopolitan high school or the elective

system. I am merely trying to indicate why we have undertaken these unique experiments in America. Schoolmasters did not deliberately decide that they would abandon the narrow, fixed curriculum which was sanctioned by tradition. They were compelled by the conditions of life around them to do something other than that which was done in this country as recently as a generation ago and is now done in countries where the social situation is less dynamic than it is in America.

The evolution of the cosmopolitan high school is clearly illustrated in the experience of Cleveland, Ohio. The original secondary schools of that city were of the traditional academic type, devoted to the preparation of pupils for college and administering a classical-mathematical curriculum. As the population of the city increased through the development of industries, the demand

for a new type of curriculum began to express itself. This demand took an extreme form, as radical demands often do.
Parents and pupils asked for courses as
different as possible from those given in
the traditional academic school. Cleveland organized a technical high school in
response to this demand. It was the expectation of those who secured the es-
tablishment of this new school that it
would give a practical education to boys
who were going to become workers in the
trades. Large numbers of pupils entered
the new technical high school. What did
they and their parents then demand?
Nothing less than an all-inclusive education. The outcome of this experiment
was, and is, that the technical high
school of Cleveland is a cosmopolitan
high school, responsive in a very high
degree to the demand for educational opportunities in many lines. The technical
school offers, in fact, almost all the ad-

vantages offered by the academic school and at the same time provides many elaborate courses in shop-work and related subjects which are unknown in the older school. What happened in Cleveland has been happening in many of the school systems in the country.

I referred to the cosmopolitan high school as an experiment. There are many influences which surround this experiment and act as checks to prevent it from becoming unmanageable. In the first place, a cosmopolitan high school is expensive. Costs mount in proportion as the program of instruction expands. In the second place, there is a kind of competition among the subjects of instruction which prevents unproductive studies from becoming permanent factors in the curriculum. In the third place, new subjects can be introduced only when teachers can be found who are competent to teach them, and teachers do not train themselves in any large numbers for subjects that are without justification.

It is difficult to sympathize with the terror which seems to possess some of the critics of the high school who look for its dissolution because of the variety of subjects of instruction which it provides. We live in an age when an effort is being made to intellectualize every kind of undertaking. What used to be bookkeeping has expanded under the conditions of modern business into the profession of accounting. Various forms of engineering have appeared in the list of professions because each requires long and arduous preparation as a prerequisite of success. Industry is in the hands of trained engineers. We might go on citing examples which show that high grades of intelligence and superior training are required in a hundred positions in society where formerly the professions were only three in number. How can anyone con-

template this expansion of intellectual
interests in society without recognizing
that the schools also must expand? The
experiment of developing an enriched
curriculum cannot, of course, be brought
to complete success in a day, but the experiment must go forward. In some way
or other the breadth of training must
correspond to legitimate modern demands.

I dare say that, if all those who object
to the American plan of education were
heard, the number of those who find the
cosmopolitan high school undesirable
would be less than the number of those
who think of the elective system as the
climax of pedagogical iniquity.

A recent critic of American education
has selected the combinations of courses
for graduation from high school and college as the target for his most caustic
ridicule. I am about to quote what he
says, but before I do so I take the liberty

of directing attention to the fact that there is a lack of coherence in this critic's writing. He starts out to describe the curriculum but becomes confused in his ideas and discusses faulty teaching and various other matters which have very little to do with the sequence of courses, that is, with the curriculum.

I quote at length from Bulletin Number Twenty of the Carnegie Foundation for the Advancement of Teaching, entitled, *The Quality of the Educational Process in the United States and in Europe.* In this bulletin the author, William S. Learned, writes as follows:

The curriculum is a rope of sand, without texture or organization. Effective education through related ideas is thereby sacrificed to the mere registering of information. This fact will be made clearer later by comparison with genuine curricula. Convinced that knowledge is power, we have assumed that presenting information is identical with conferring knowledge, and have hastened to make broad this easy and royal road to an educated democracy. Information on almost any subject can easily be formulated into convenient units. And it is possible for a mind even of very limited powers, if socially docile, and inspired by filial duty, personal pride, commercial advantage, or any one of a dozen other extraneous motives, to take in and give out this information in recognizable word or paraphrase without seriously knowing or caring what it is all about. This is positively all that the school, and usually the college, requires, and of this it asks but a fraction — 60 per cent. For fear of evaporation the process is checked up at once — daily recitation, written review, monthly test, and term examination. These concluded, responsibility ceases, and "credit" is recorded, of which no future misstep, even though it discloses total ignorance, can ever deprive the pupil.

Zeal for our broad, trunk-line school, where every child of democracy may come and choose the information that most attracts him, has blinded us to the fact that "power" disappears under such a régime. The knowledge that is power presupposes a mind actively at work and bent on the process of self-education. Such a mind requires the meanings and relations of its information, and finds little advancement in minute and disconnected masses of fact that must, from the nature of our system, stand neatly alone. Instead of developing an agency to attend, supply, and encourage a pupil who is using his own mind, we have done our best to devise a vehicle that will *carry* the minds of as many as choose to get on board. To graduate from either high school or college today may hardly be rated as, of itself, an intellectual achievement. It is at best a moderately worthy exhibition of certain moral qualities. [pp. 5–6]

The writer of the foregoing paragraphs can hardly find words in which to express his admiration of the coherence which he says is characteristic of all European schools. He would have America repent and go back to the path of rectitude indicated by the example of Europe.

Before quoting from Mr. Learned's bulletin, I pointed out that there is a difference between a poor curriculum and the kind of inefficient teaching which he seems to regard as inevitable in schools organized as are American schools. If it were true that our schools are guilty of every sin that Mr. Learned catalogues, it would not follow that we ought to go back to the European curriculum, and it would not follow that a reversion would save our educational lives. There have not been lacking in the history of schools cases in which Caesar has been badly taught and in which geometry has been treated by inferior teachers as a collection of isolated propositions. On the other hand, we have all seen, I am sure, the most stimulating instruction given to young minds by a teacher of biology or some other subject, who is thoroughly familiar with his field. Such a teacher often produces a profound impression even though he has the class under his supervision for only a single semester. There is a coherence that results from daily interest in a line of thinking which opens up a new world of thought. This

is totally different from the coherence
which results from repetitious drill. A
curriculum cannot be a "rope of sand"
if it is administered by teachers whose
thinking is logical and consecutive.

It is, I am sure, hardly worth the time
of this company to listen at any length to
an exchange of opinions between two ob-
servers of European teaching who are in
utter disagreement. I cannot refrain,
however, from making a record of the
fact that I have seen in German *Gymnasien* teaching as poor as any I ever
witnessed. A few years ago, as a repre-
sentative of the United States Bureau of
Education, I had an unusual opportunity
to visit classes in Germany which are not
ordinarily open to visitors. Anyone who
makes sweeping and unqualified statements about the universal excellence of
German teaching may find acceptance as
a competent witness among large groups
of my countrymen, but he will have to be

satisfied with my rejection of his testimony, however little that rejection may distress him. I visited some of the classes which were not the first choices of the principals, and I arrived at the conclusion that superficial students of the German system are not invited into classes where the German system is encountering difficulties.

I am prepared, as a result of personal observation, to bear similar testimony with regard to English schools. I shall have to plead guilty to personal ignorance concerning the French *lycées*. I have read, however, that there has been not a little effort in recent years to reform the curriculum of the *lycées*. Apparently, the French people are not as certain as are some of their American visitors of the unqualified excellence of what is being done in their secondary schools. I am disposed to believe that the writer who reviewed Mr. Learned's book in the London *Times Educational Supplement* was right when he said that Mr. Learned had "deliberately attempted to contrast American education at its worst with European education at its best."

Returning to the main topic, we must keep vividly in mind the principle that no solution of our American problem will ever be reached by retracing our steps. The world has never before seen an experiment in the evolution of a flexible, elective secondary-school program. No other country has ever attempted on such a scale as has the United States to raise the level of commercial and industrial undertakings by supplying a universal higher education. Vituperation of the American program is as useless as vilification of the sunrise. If anyone can tell us how to make the American secondary school more flexible, he will be recognized as a leader. Any author who exhorts us to stop in the midst of our ex-

periment and put the high school into a
strait-jacket has chosen his own place
among the writers of curious documents,
valuable only as additions to the collec-
tions of antiquarians.

I would not have you misinterpret my
plea for flexibility as an abandonment of
the hope for coherence. There is a coherence which results from holding
rigidly to a restricted range of ideas. The
fact that a pupil is taught nationalistic
history yesterday, today, and tomorrow
may leave on his mind the impression
that nationalistic history is highly important — more important, indeed, than
anything else in the field of history.
Such a repetitious program, which, by
the way, is to be found in every European school, may serve to keep the thinking of pupils rotating about the same
problems, may foster a certain type of
conviction about one's own country and
about its boundaries and enemies, and

may supply coherence without advantage and continuity without intellectual illumination. He who advocates coherence through repetition is an unsafe guide.

There is evidence that our flexible American program is evolving a new thing, namely, a coherence in school studies which results not from dull repetition but from an apprehension of the fact that genuine learning aids the individual to adapt himself to his social obligations.

Let me illustrate what I mean by reference to a particular case. I know the record of a boy who entered the high school with the idea that ultimately he would follow some commercial pursuit. He elected in his freshman year the commercial courses which were offered in arithmetic and geography. Through these studies he became interested in the broader principles which govern industrial and commercial relations. He was led to study some of the sciences during his second year. Stimulated by his contacts with these fields of knowledge, he began to think of going to college. Finding that it is conventional to lay emphasis on literary and mathematical courses in preparation for college, he devoted the last two years of the four which he spent in high school to the study of foreign languages and mathematics. Anyone who looks at the record of this boy will note at once that he wandered about among the offerings of the high school. Anyone interested primarily in statistics who finds a hundred records of pupils shifting from commerce to science and from science to the classics probably can justify his criticism of American education at least far enough to satisfy those who prefer to set up a social system where there are no lines of migration from business to intellectual pursuits.

Anyone, on the other hand, who is interested in intellectual awakenings, who finds the finest type of coherence in genuine mental development rather than in tabulated records can hardly fail to recognize in the progress of the boy whom I have described an exhibition of the American type of coherence as contrasted with the European type.

It is not argued here that every American pupil achieves in his intellectual life that coherence which makes all kinds of knowledge part of a well-integrated development, but it is argued that the experiment of arousing American youth is under way in a form that is unique and far too successful to be abandoned.

Even those who demand the type of continuity which results from the pursuit of similar subjects year after year will find not a little in the programs of American schools which shows that under proper conditions secondary-school curriculums of individual pupils are consecutive in every sense of the word. One needs only to read the requirements for graduation prescribed by the state board of education in such a state as California to realize that the statements of the critics of American high schools about the lack of sequential courses are far from true. It is a fact that in the great majority of high schools the administrators can be trusted to interest themselves intelligently in the development of pupils, and they are near enough to the individual cases to be more competent in selecting courses for pupils than are those who deal with the high school at long range and with no regard for the social conditions in the midst of which this institution does its work.

I find my own thinking greatly stimulated not only by the breadth of the American curriculum but also and especially by certain new courses which are being tried in a number of American high schools. Let us consider briefly a typical example. In Rochester (New York), Detroit (Michigan), Richmond (Indiana), Los Angeles (California), and other cities teachers of language have seen the possibility of introducing pupils to the romantic field of comparative philology by means of a general-language course. Instead of expecting young people to spend their time gleaning a few ideas about the cultures of antiquity through the intensive study of a limited number of pages of a single author, these teachers of language have sought out striking examples of the relation between human thought and human modes of expressing thought. They are introducing pupils to new and highly productive ideas about the way in which the human mind has evolved. They are making pupils conscious of the beauty and simplicity of the English language. In short, they are teaching more about language in a semester than pupils could discover in a lifetime by the methods of drill followed in schools which have never realized the possibility of making school work coherent by making it interesting and informing.

Those of us who are optimistic about the American attempt to develop the productive type of teaching which is necessary if the elective system is to succeed cannot listen with any patience to the plea for a curriculum which includes four years of Latin because, forsooth, Cicero has traditionally followed Caesar, and Vergil has brought up the rear of the procession. There is a certain progression from Latin to Latin in such a sequence, it is true, but there is no guaranty that this progression will result in enthusiasm for the rational solution of the pupils' intellectual problems. It is quite as thinkable that a boy will become intellectually mature from the study of

civics and economics, and it is certainly
not outside the probabilities that civics
and economics will hold his attention
more firmly than will the poetry of
Vergil.

Whether one is optimistic or pessimis-
tic about the American program of secondary education, that program is here,
and there is not the slightest indication
that it is going to revert to the European
form of education. Quite the contrary.
The expansion of the American program
and its flexibility are being imitated in
Europe. There is an interest in other
countries in the American type of education that is reflected in official reports
and incidental discussions. There is a
hope among the citizens of every other
land that some day higher education
may be both open to their children, as
it is to the children on this continent,
and appropriate to the needs of each
child.

Some years ago I went to a meeting of a labor union in an English city. The purpose of the meeting was the announcement of some courses which had been provided by the city board of education for adults. I listened with interest to the talks given by the leaders of the union. One of them, inspired perhaps by the presence of an American, used a phrase which I shall not forget. He commented on the increasing educational advantages that were being provided for the common people of England. Using a phrase coined by Matthew Arnold, he expressed his gratification that an increasing number of the children of the common people could enjoy the advantages of a secondary education because they were able to scale the "educational ladder." He paused on the words "educational ladder" and said, "I hope the time will come when we shall have in England not an educational ladder but an educational stairway, such as they have in the United States."

Up to this point I have attempted to show that the American high school is characterized by accessibility and flexibility. Let us turn now to a third characteristic. The American high school has one quality that even its most unfriendly critics recognize as unique — it has huge size. I do not refer to individual schools although some of these rival in size universities of the first rank. I refer, rather, to the high-school system as a whole. I shall not review here the statistics of the pupil population of secondary schools. The matter of size is relevant to our present discussion because size inevitably results in certain consequences which we must understand if we are to have a full comprehension of the experiment in which we are engaged.

The teaching staff of any educational institution is its most essential item of equipment. Providing suitable teachers for American high schools is a task so colossal that our civilization is staggered in its efforts to meet the demand. There are some who comment adversely on the training of the teachers in the high schools and use phrases which seem to indicate that the schools are in some sense guilty of deliberate neglect. The fact is that the schools are increasing so rapidly in the number of pupils enrolled that the generation which has completed its education is not able to supply teachers in adequate numbers. In 1925 there were 155,000 teachers in the public secondary schools of the United States. This is more by 30,000 than the total number of graduates of the colleges of the country in a year. When one thinks of the other occupations and professions which college graduates enter, one realizes the difficulty of recruiting the teaching staffs of the high schools even if nothing more were demanded than graduation from college.

The problem which confronts the country can be described in another way. If every accredited high school and every college in the United States had a single well-trained mathematician on its staff, there would be somewhat more than twenty thousand well-trained mathematicians in the United States. When one thinks of the mathematicians who are needed in the industries and in commerce and estimates this number as perhaps equal to the number required by the schools, one begins to realize that civilization itself is subjected to the severest test. Are there forty thousand persons in a generation who are sufficiently interested in mathematics and sufficiently competent in this specialty to provide what the country needs?

Our ability or inability to provide

competent teachers will determine the success or failure of the American experiment of universal secondary education. We may be able to tolerate for a time partly trained teachers. We have developed certain devices in this country which very ingeniously cover up some of our deficiencies. We put textbooks into the hands of teachers and pupils and depend on these to supply a very large share of the method as well as the content of class exercises. Some years ago H. G. Wells made the comment that the devices for making good teachers out of mediocre individuals will have to be multiplied. There are so few good teachers, he pointed out, that the genius of these few must be conserved in some fashion and must be made available to pupils who cannot enjoy personal contact with them. He recommended that the best physics teachers give demonstrations before motion-picture cameras and that the photographs thus secured be used in classrooms presided over by those who are less competent. He would use phonographs and printed materials in the fields in which motion pictures cannot serve the purpose.

I have no simple formula to suggest by which the need for an adequate supply of highly competent high-school teachers can be met. I am quite sure of one fact. There is no justification for accusing the schools of neglect. The schools are now held in check by political and financial influences which render it well-nigh impossible for them to carry the load which the ambitions of pupils and parents impose upon them. Many an administrative officer who is charged with the conduct of a secondary school would gladly devote his energy to securing teachers of higher grade than his present resources will permit, but he is confronted with the task of keeping the

taxpayers who support his institution
sufficiently satisfied so that they will not
reduce his budget. Even if the budge-
tary difficulty were removed, the human
problem remains. Is the present generation competent to provide for the complete training of the next?

I do not belong to the group of students of school administration who believe that the problem of supplying
teachers is primarily a financial problem. Like all members of the profession,
I am glad to see the salaries of teachers
increased, but I am persuaded that the
supply of high-grade teachers will always be limited. For my own part, I am
willing to see our educational procedures
modified so as to bring more pupils in
contact with those who are most efficient
in inspiring pupils to study. I consider
the investigations which are being made
with regard to the possibility of ma-
terially increasing the sizes of classes as

among the most promising lines of inquiry now being pursued in our educational system.

Furthermore, I believe we shall have to depend increasingly on independent work on the part of pupils. In short, the conservation of instructional genius seems to me to be one of the most urgent necessities of our times. On the negative side, it cannot be too emphatically pointed out that curtailment of educational opportunity by elimination of pupils is certainly not the formula that should be adopted. If there are too few well-trained teachers now, it is a suicidal policy to limit the pupil population in the hope of keeping the demand down to the inadequate supply. A policy of expansion rather than a policy of repression must be devised.

The sheer magnitude of the secondary-school enterprise in this country has not only brought us face to face with the

grave problem of providing a suitable
staff but has also raised the question of
the possibility of material support. How
is the country to house all the pupils?
How is space to be secured, especially in
the congested sections of cities? How are
laboratories and gymnasiums to be provided? I remember a conversation which
I had some years ago with an English
educator who was fully informed about
American conditions. I refer to Sir
Michael Sadler. He had been good
enough to help me become acquainted
with the flourishing secondary and
higher municipal institutions of Leeds.
I asked him why English cities did not
make secondary schools free, for I had
observed unbounded enthusiasm for the
new municipal secondary schools. "We
cannot afford it," he replied. Then he
added, "You cannot afford what you are
doing either, but you do not know it
yet." I hope that Sir Michael is wrong.

I am confident that he is, but I am quite sure that, if the American public has to maintain a secondary-school system larger than the present system, there will have to be a strict and convincing accounting by those who are in charge of the experiment.

From the consideration of the size of the high school, I turn to comment on what, for want of a better term, I shall designate as "pupil spirit." There is a kind of flippancy in the American youth which is very trying to some of our intellectuals. American young people seem to take the high school for granted and think of it as one of Nature's free gifts. The ordinary boy or girl is wholly unaware of the fact that the high school is one of the most expensive and most daring social experiments of our day. There is a very different attitude among the pupils in European secondary schools. In those schools it is

recognized as a privilege to attend. No
German boy ever treats lightly his mem-
bership in a *Gymnasium*. The adverse
judgment of three instructors excludes a
boy from that institution, and adverse
judgments are rendered in such numbers
that the pupil mortality is very high.
When a boy is excluded from the *Gymnasium*, he understands that the avenues
of social preferment are closed to him.

Here again I draw the contrast not for
the purpose of advocating imitation but
for the purpose of throwing light on our
experiment. It would be altogether dis-
advantageous to increase the ratio of
pupil mortality in American schools as a
means of convincing boys and girls that
the opportunity to gain a high-school
education is a privilege to be highly
prized. There must be some American
way of providing a substitute for the
tension which pervades the European
secondary schools. There must be some

way to secure the coöperation of the pupils themselves in developing in this country an attitude of regard for intellectual life which shall be more explicit and more general than is the present attitude. There is vaguely in the minds of all Americans a respect for education. That is the reason why parents make sacrifices and pupils flock into the schools. This vague notion needs to be cultivated and made into a vivid, conscious recognition of the meaning of what is going on in the unique high schools of the United States.

I advocate direct instruction in the meaning and value of American opportunities. I do this the more earnestly because I believe that the next generation is certain to go farther than we have gone in developing educational opportunities for all classes of people. I am sure that the proper evolution of the high school as a public institution requires a thoughtful consideration of the characteristics of American life, and I am driven to the conclusion that such thoughtful consideration has, up to this time, been less common than it should be. If this were the proper time and place, that statement could, I think, be expanded, and it could be shown that there is need of instruction in order to secure a general understanding of American institutions other than the schools. I am advocating the injection into the school curriculum of a course or series of courses intended to make young people aware of the peculiarities of American life. I should be willing to give a hearing in such a course to reports on European institutions if only those reports could be made somewhat more accurate than are the writings regarding European schools to which I have had occasion to refer. Without attempting to dictate in full the content or method of a course in American institutions, I advocate its introduction into the curriculum with all the emphasis that I can command.

The statement just made leads to a discussion of a final fact with regard to the American high school which must always be kept in mind by anyone who attempts to understand this institution. The high school, in common with all educational institutions in this country, is controlled by the people of the locality in which it is situated. Local control of the high school is more complete than is local control of the elementary school or college. Elementary schools have for some decades past been increasingly brought under the guidance of state departments of public instruction, and American colleges are governed by trustees who are usually chosen from a relatively wide area. The high schools are supervised comparatively little by state departments, and even the superintendent of public schools in most municipalities is timid about attempting to direct the program of secondary education.

Local control of the secondary schools is one of the most striking characteristics of our American system. In Germany, while the states have jurisdiction over the lower schools, the federal authorities control the *Gymnasien*. In France central control of the *lycées* is like the German control of the *Gymnasien* — absolute. In England there is a degree of local autonomy, but central control operates to an extent unknown in this country. In the countries where central control exists, it is readily possible by the exercise of power to produce conformity to certain fixed standards. It is possible to prevent the existence of certain deficiencies which arise in America, where the ambition of communities outruns their intelligence. Fixity and uniformity have been very generally achieved in

European secondary schools. The opposite is true in the United States. One can find in this country every possible kind of high school. Anyone who tries to make a general statement regarding American high schools immediately finds that there are more exceptions to his statement than there are cases of agreement with his description. There is no such institution as a typical American high school.

During the past three decades there have arisen in the various sections of the United States voluntary organizations in the councils of which representatives of the secondary schools and colleges of the region meet to discuss ways and means of improving the schools. These organizations are guided by standards which they have adopted. There is no governmental dictation and no dogmatic insistence on standards which have artificial and unchallengeable authority. The type of standardization which is effected through voluntary coöperation is much more in keeping with American habits of thought than would be any type derived from governmental authority.

It is one of the finest virtues of the American educational system that, while it is free to develop according to the needs of each locality, it is impelled by its own devotion to the rational solution of problems to cultivate as its guide a body of scientifically established principles. Local control, which seems at first sight to be a loose and unpromising method of guiding education, has made so manifest the need of educational science that America has become in a unique sense the home of this science. However extravagant the praise heaped on Old World institutions by writers who would have us imitate Europe, there has never been any possibility of urging America to adopt European methods of control.

There has never been a writer bold enough to attempt the fiction that Europe has a science of education.

Unfortunately, the science of education cannot be reported as in full control of American schools. In a democracy we are constantly reminded of the fact that there are forces other than reason which operate in educational systems to determine policies and practices. It would be gratifying at times if some of our prostrate municipalities could confess their intellectual bankruptcy and could go into the hands of almost any receiver who would accept the task of bringing them back to sane modes of living and efficient methods of conducting their schools. This easy method of meeting the obligations of democracy is, however, out of the question. For better or for worse, we have local control. Some day we shall learn how to use the power which is in our hands, and we shall have a school system that is adapted to our needs because it has been developed in the closest relation to these needs. At the same time our system will not be as provincial as it is now because educational science has devised a terminology which makes it possible for local systems to communicate with one another and because there are exact methods of measurement which make it possible to institute revealing comparisons of the effectiveness of the educational devices that originate in widely separated systems.

The history of the American school system is a history of gradual accumulation of wisdom and of gradual perfection of organization. We certainly have defects which must be cured, but there is only one way to cure these defects, that is, by pushing forward along the lines which have been determined by our own unique evolution.

As I bring my tribute of respect to Alexander Inglis, I deem it fitting to seek reinforcement of what I have said by appeal to his attitude and to his writings. He always sought by the most searching inquiry to understand the educational situations with which he dealt. He was never guilty of false portrayal for the sake of literary effect or because of lack of careful inquiry. He first surveyed the field with diligence and with all the paraphernalia of the science of education, to which he was a large contributor. Having discovered the facts, he had the courage to suggest new experiments. I recall how he responded to the invitation of one of our middle western states to give assistance in the construction of a high-school curriculum for the semi-rural districts. It was his spirit of fearless attack on new problems which made him a leader among us.

In the course of my preparation of this paper, I read once more his masterly discussion of American secondary education. If I were not an optimist in my own right, I am very sure I should be an optimist by contagion. Professor Inglis' book is no weak, carping criticism, no false caricature; it is the work of a writer who knew the virtues of the unique institution which has been erected within our American educational system. To be sure, he also recognized clearly the problems which the school must solve in the future. There is in his writing no evasion of these problems, no platitudinous reference to what we might be if we were something else. There is a straightforward wholesome discussion, which has helped a generation to see more clearly and to act more wisely.

I think it is fair to classify our former colleague as an expansionist. He did not

at any point propose to abandon the experiment of universal secondary education. He did not advocate the abandonment of the elective system. He did not
favor a contraction of the curriculum.
On the contrary, he was strong in his ap-
peals for enlargement of opportunity
and for adjustment to the needs of the
individual. He was a contributor to
educational science through the syste-
matic measurement of results.

I am content to follow the path that
he took. I believe in a system of secondary education which has universal accessibility and maximum flexibility. I
believe that we should put forth in this
country all the energy we can command
in the effort to supply the oncoming generation with the most stimulating ideas
that we can offer. I believe that this
duty will be most fully discharged by en-
riching the curriculum. I do not believe

that the highest form of training is secured through mere sequential drill. I believe that it is possible to stimulate the minds of pupils to independent thinking and that such thinking is the highest achievement of an educational institution. I believe in local control guided by science. Above all, I believe in giving the people of this country a clear idea of the virtues and advantages of our educational system. I believe that a discussion of American problems can be carried on in such a way that the young people in the schools will have a true idea of their privileges and opportunities and the public will be willing to support adequately the experiment of universal secondary education.

In this faith, I am confident that it is the duty of all who are aware of the magnitude and importance of this enterprise to turn away from trivial criticism and from speculation as to possible abandonment of the present type of organization and to use all the energy that is available in bringing into the present system the most highly trained leaders that can be provided.